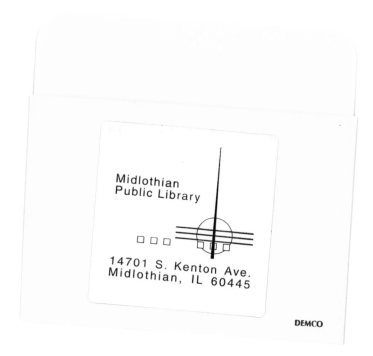

Pebble® Plus

Sports and Activities
Let's Play Football!

by Jan Mader

Consulting Editor: Gail Saunders-Smith, PhD

Consultant: Kymm Ballard, MA
Physical Education, Athletics, and Sports Medicine Consultant
North Carolina Department of Public Instruction

Capstone press®

Mankato, Minnesota

Pebble Plus is published by Capstone Press,
151 Good Counsel Drive, P.O. Box 669, Mankato, Minnesota 56002.
www.capstonepress.com

1 2 3 4 5 6 11 10 09 08 07 06

Library of Congress Cataloging-in-Publication Data
Mader, Jan.
    Let's play football / by Jan Mader.
    p. cm.—(Pebble plus. Sports and activities)
    Summary: "Simple text and photographs present the skills, equipment, and safety concerns of
football"—Provided by publisher.
    Includes bibliographical references and index.
    ISBN-13: 978-0-7368-6361-2 (hardcover)
    ISBN-10: 0-7368-6361-3 (hardcover)
    1. Football—Juvenile literature. I. Title. II. Series.
GV950.7.M25 2007
796.332—dc22   2006000500

Editorial Credits
Amber Bannerman, editor; Juliette Peters, set designer; Bobbi J. Wyss, book designer; Kelly Garvin, photo
    researcher/photo editor

Photo Credits
Capstone Press/Karon Dubke, 10–11 (football); TJ Thoraldson Digital Photography, cover, 1 (kids with football),
    5, 8–9, 13, 19 (player)
Corbis/Kelly-Mooney Photography, 14–15; Michael Kim, 16–17; Michael Prince, 18–19 (background);
    Tom Stewart, 21
Getty Images Inc./John Giustina, 6–7
Photodisc, 1 (clouds)
Shutterstock/Greg Soybelman, 10–11 (goalposts)

Note to Parents and Teachers

The Sports and Activities set supports national physical education standards related
to recognizing movement forms and exhibiting a physically active lifestyle. This book
describes and illustrates football. The images support early readers in understanding the
text. The repetition of words and phrases helps early readers learn new words. This book
also introduces early readers to subject-specific vocabulary words, which are defined in
the Glossary section. Early readers may need assistance to read some words and to use
the Table of Contents, Glossary, Read More, Internet Sites, and Index sections of the book.

Table of Contents

Playing Football

Punt, pass, run, tackle!

Toss the football

with your friends.

One team runs and passes

down the field.

The other team

tries to stop them.

Players get the ball

to the end zone.

Touchdown!

They score six points.

Players kick the ball through

the goalposts.

They score three points.

Field goal!

Football Equipment

Footballs are made of
strong brown leather.
White laces help players
hold on to the ball.

Football fields have
many white lines.
Goalposts stand at
each end of the field.

Football Safety

Helmets protect players' heads
from tackles and hits.
Mouth guards protect
their teeth.

Thick pads keep

players' bodies safe.

Shoes with cleats help keep

players from slipping.

Having Fun

Come kick, run, score,

and cheer.

Let's play football!

Glossary

cleats—small tips on the bottom of shoes that help players stop or turn quickly

end zone—the area at the end of the field; when a team gets the ball into the end zone, they score a touchdown.

field goal—a three-point score in a football game

goalpost—a post that marks each end of the field; players get points for getting the ball through the goalposts.

protect—to keep safe

punt—a kick where the ball is dropped from the hands and kicked before it touches the ground

tackle—to stop another player by knocking them to the ground

touchdown—a six-point score in a football game

Read More

Goin, Kenn. *Football for Fun!*. Sports for Fun!. Minneapolis: Compass Point Books, 2003.

Klingel, Cynthia Fitterer, and Robert B. Noyed. *Football*. Wonder Books. Chanhassen, Minn.: Child's World, 2003.

Internet Sites

FactHound offers a safe, fun way to find Internet sites related to this book. All of the sites on FactHound have been researched by our staff.

Here's how:

1. Visit *www.facthound.com*

2. Choose your grade level.

3. Type in this book ID **0736863613** for age-appropriate sites. You may also browse subjects by clicking on letters, or by clicking on pictures and words.

4. Click on the **Fetch It** button.

FactHound will fetch the best sites for you!

Index

Word Count: 117
Grade: 1
Early-Intervention Level: 14